Be Encouraged Through Prayer

Be Encouraged Through Prayer

Be Encouraged In Your Prayer Life

Dr. Kettely Doxy

XULON PRESS

Xulon Press
2301 Lucien Way #415
Maitland, FL 32751
407.339.4217
www.xulonpress.com

© 2020 by Dr. Kettely Doxy

Photo credit: Woodline Dorcin Photography

All rights reserved solely by the author. The author guarantees all contents are original and do not infringe upon the legal rights of any other person or work. No part of this book may be reproduced in any form without the permission of the author. The views expressed in this book are not necessarily those of the publisher.

Unless otherwise indicated, Scripture quotations taken from the Holy Bible, New International Version (NIV). Copyright © 1973, 1978, 1984, 2011 by Biblica, Inc.™. Used by permission. All rights reserved.

Printed in the United States of America.

ISBN-13: 978-1-6312-9005-3

Table of Contents

Acknowledgement..............................vii

Dear Readers:.................................ix

1-What is Prayer?..............................1

2-What Does Prayer Look Like in the Bible?..........3

The Attitude And Motives Of The Person Who Prayed .. 13

Acknowledgement

First and foremost, praises and thanks be to GOD, the Almighty, for His showers of blessings throughout my writing project to complete this book successfully.

I would like to express my deep and sincere gratitude to my husband (Rev. Dr. Emmanes Doxy) for providing invaluable guidance throughout my writing project, I am also grateful for what he has offered me. I am extending my heartfelt thanks to my children (Lily, Stephen, Emmanuel) for their love, prayers and support.

My special thanks goes to my Church family and Ms. Christelle J Bourdeau for their keen interest shown to complete this book successfully.

Dear Readers:

I declare God's incredible blessings over your life. You will see an explosion of God's goodness, with sudden, widespread increase. You will experience the surpassing greatness of God's favor. You will be elevated to a level higher than you ever dreamed of. Explosive blessings are coming your way. For the many phases of life I went through, I can say prayer is the breath of life. When you stop praying, life ceases; it is important to go to God for everything. I don't wait for trouble; I pray constantly and spontaneously because life is rough, but God is good.

When we pray…
-We experienced love, hope, joy, and patience
-God hears us and He will answer
-We obtain forgiveness
-Everything changes
-Mountains disappeared
-Countless blessings without asking God
-Access in the presence of God
-Healing and deliverance are taking place
-Gain favor with God and men

Be Encouraged Through Prayer

-Love others
-Become stronger in the Lord
-Fruitful in the kingdom
-The mind of Christ
-Our discerning spirits are on point
-Allow God to permeate our spirits
-God does supernatural and divine
-Coincidences happened
-God provides into our bodies energy, strength, and power
-Good things will come
-See ourselves rising.

1-What is Prayer?

Prayer is the place you go to admit yourself into humility before God and hope for the best by faith; also, it's a privilege to say, "Father, I love you with all my heart through Jesus Christ." Everyone prays in their own different way; at the same time, God hears them all. When we talk to God, God will talk back to us. He will provoke us, rouse us, stir us, goad us, and prompt us because all the things we just talked to God about all the things we praised God for, all the questions, all the pain and the joy we express in prayer are founded in the truth of God. When we say "amen," it is no longer an option.

Biblical prayers have a common denominator of hope. Hope causes us to look upward and fall down on our knees, holding onto the One who sits above all. Deuteronomy 33:12 says the beloved of the Lord rest between His shoulders … they rest secure in Him. Prayer is hopeful rest and release of all physical or emotional pain that drives us into His capable arms. The Bible says in Psalm 91:5 God watches us through the night, even while we sleep. Have you ever been jolted awake at night for no apparent reason? Sometimes, just personally, I believe it is to connect with us in prayer.

2-What Does Prayer Look Like in the Bible?

At times, prayer in the Scriptures is poetic and, at other times, it is conversational, delivered through a teaching or written in a letter. Still others are meditative writings and recollections of who God is and what He's brought us through, up to this point. There are at least nine different types of prayer in the Bible: prayers of faith, corporate prayer, petitions or requests (supplication), thanksgiving, worship, dedication, intercession, imprecation, and praying in the Spirit.

David, a man after God's own heart, poured his heart out in prayer to the Father many times throughout Scripture. Whether hidden in a cave from his enemies or ashamed of his sin, David turned to God for help and for forgiveness. He praised God for who He was. His prayerful relationship with God covers many pages of the book of Psalms and stands as a reminder of how personal our God is. In the New Testament, we see Paul's intimate relationship with the Father, through his life's testimony and the prayers he prayed for the churches he planted after his encounter with Christ. He mentions prayer forty-one times.

Though they lived in very different times, hope can be heard in both David and Paul's words. It bleeds through their letters and poems so personally and profoundly. These two men were forever changed by knowing their great God.

Jesus's prayers during His earthly ministry are mentioned twenty-five times. Mark 1:35 tells of how he woke early in the morning to find a quiet place to pray to his Father. He taught us how to pray:

"Our Father in heaven, hallowed be your name, your kingdom come, your will be done, on earth as it is in heaven. Give us today our daily bread. And forgive us our debts as we also have forgiven our debtors. And lead us not into temptation, but deliver us from the evil one." (Matthew 6:9-13)

He prayed in the garden, to the point of agony, for God to lift the burden of the cross from Him. But He closed the prayer faithfully with, "not my will, but yours be done" (Luke 22:42). When we pour our hearts out to God, by Jesus's example, we cover it with God's will by praying in Jesus's name. Prayers are often ended with "Amen," which means "Very well. God has heard my prayer; this I know as a certainty and a truth."

1. The Lord's Prayer

"Our Father in heaven, hallowed be your name, your kingdom come, your will be done, on earth as it is in heaven. Give us today our daily bread. And forgive us our debts, as we also have forgiven our debtors. And lead us not into temptation, but deliver us from the evil one." (Matthew 6:9-13)

There's something very powerful in praying the words Jesus spoke. Jesus taught us to address God's rightful place as the Father, worship and praise God for who He is and all He has done. Because of Christ's death and resurrection, we are forgiven of our sins when we confess and repent, and may petition God for His protection and help. When we don't have the words to pray, we can turn to the Lord's prayer and ask the Holy Spirit to help us personalize it to our daily lives. Paraphrased in The Message translation, it reads: "This is your Father in heaven you are dealing with, and he knows better than you and what you need. With a God like this loving you, you can pray very simply."

WE All can Learn from The Prayer Life Of Jesus

Luke 11:1 (NIV) reads, "One day Jesus was praying in a certain place. When he finished, one of his disciples said to him, 'Lord, teach us to pray, just as John taught his disciples.'" [1] There's much to learn from this passage beyond the significant Lord's Prayer that follows it. For one, we learn that what sparked the unnamed disciple's curiosity to learn about prayer was the fact that he saw Jesus in prayer. We also learn that John the Baptist taught his disciples to pray and, as a result, the disciples of Jesus were also interested in learning to pray, or at least one of them was! Isn't it interesting that out of all the disciples, only one of them asked Jesus to teach them to pray? It sometimes seems the church is in a similar situation today regarding prayer. We talk about prayer, we study prayer, we say our prayers, but how many of us actually seek earnestly for God to teach us to pray?

Jesus prayed for others: In Matthew 19:13, we read, "Then little children were brought to Jesus for him to place his hands on them and pray for them." Despite the fact that "the disciples rebuked those who brought them," Jesus said the children should not be hindered "for the kingdom of heaven belongs to such as these" (v. 14). In John 17:9, we read, "I [Jesus] pray for them. I am not praying for the world, but for those you have given Me, for they are Yours." This underscores the need for intercessory prayer. *Jesus prayed with others:* Luke 9:28 reads, "[Jesus] took Peter, John and James with Him and went up onto a mountain to pray." Jesus prayed alone, as we'll read below, but He also knew the value of praying with others. Acts 1:14 underscores the importance of Christians praying with one another: "They all joined together constantly in prayer ..." *Jesus prayed alone:* Luke 5:16 reads, "But Jesus often withdrew to lonely places and prayed." As much as Jesus understood the value of praying with and for others, He also understood the need to pray alone. Psalm 46:10 reads, "Be still, and know that I am God." Sometimes it's important for us to "be still" before God, but the only way to do this, especially in our hectic culture, is to do so alone with God. *Jesus prayed in nature:* Psalm 19:1 reads, "The heavens declare the glory of God; the skies proclaim the work of his hands." What better place to commune with our Creator than among the wonders of nature? Luke 6:12 says, "One of those days Jesus went out to a mountainside to pray ..." He could have gone to a home, a synagogue, or, if He were near Jerusalem, He could have gone to the temple to pray. But there were times when Jesus made the decision to pray where He was, which often happened to be in nature.

When Jesus prayed in the Garden of Gethsemane, "Yet not as I will, but as You will," He offered a tremendous but seemingly simple insight into prayer: God is in charge. As we learn from the prayer life of Jesus – and there is much to learn – we need to keep this overarching principle in mind. A disciple asked Jesus, "Lord, teach us to pray," (Luke 11:1) and, in response, was taught the Lord's Prayer. But by studying the prayer life of Jesus, we can learn not only the important truths of the Lord's Prayer but so much more. *Robert Velarde is author of* Conversations with C.S. Lewis

(InterVarsity Press), The Heart of Narnia *(NavPress), and primary author of* The Power of Family Prayer *(National Day of Prayer Task Force). Focus on the Family January 1, 2008* Unless otherwise noted all Scripture quotations are from the New International Version of the Bible.

2. Mary's Prayer

And Mary said: "My soul glorifies the Lord and my spirit rejoices in God my Savior, for he has been mindful of the humble state of his servant. From now on all generations will call me blessed, for the Mighty One has done great things for me- holy is his name. His mercy extended to those who fear him, from generation to generation. He has performed mighty deeds with his arm; he has scattered those who are proud in their inmost thoughts. He has brought down rulers from their thrones but has lifted up the humble. He has filled the hungry with good things but has sent the rich away empty. He has helped his servant Israel, remembering to be merciful to Abraham and his descendants forever, just as he promised our ancestors." (Luke 1:46-55)

Mary's song is known as "The Magnificat." Mary was humbled and overcome with joy by the way God saw her and chose her as the earthly mother of Jesus. Her prayer reflects her admiration for God. So much of our prayer life is consumed by requests and worries. Rightly so, as the world is broken and pressing in on our lives daily with new fears and anxieties. It's easy to feel invisible, even in a world more connected by technology than ever.

Mary's prayer reminds us of the importance in taking time to remember who God is, and that He sees us. All of us; the lowest of the low. He sees even the tiniest of problems that cause us even a hint of sadness. He is close to us and compassionate. Contrary to what society would have us believe, all is well and good with God. Spend time with Him and you will obtain big dividends.

3. The Prayer of Jabez

> *"Jabez cried out to the God of Israel, 'Oh that you would bless me and enlarge my territory! Let your hand be with me, and keep me from harm so that I will be free from pain.' And God granted his request"* (Chronicles 4:10).

To pray like Jabez is to submit our lives to God as a blank cloth. In the Old Testament, we find Jabez's prayer; his name literally means *pain*! He prayed for God to deliver Him from his namesake. Oh, how we fight who we are sometimes. Materialistic gain is not the point and purpose of Jabez's prayer, but rather an expansion of the heart. God promises us provision, not prosperity.

God created each person with a unique purpose and place amidst the people that surround our everyday lives. When we pray, it's important to stay open to the type of territory God wills to expand and enlarge in our lives. First and foremost is the growth of godly knowledge and spiritual gifts in our hearts. He will lead us into our purposes, as we obediently repent of our sins and pursue Jesus Christ. We were meant to honor Him in all we do and with all we have.

How You Can Use Prayer Examples in the Bible to Strengthen Your Prayer Life

There are many amazing prayers in the book of Psalms that give us words to pray when we don't know what to say. Psalm 86 is one of many in which David pours his heart out to God. In it, he prays, "Hear me, LORD, and answer me, for

I am poor and needy. Guard my life, for I am faithful to you; save your servant who trusts in you. You are my God; have mercy on me, Lord, for I call to you all day long. Bring joy to your servant, Lord, for I put my trust in you" (vv 1-4).

David, though his life and experiences on this earth, is vastly different from our modern set of circumstances, but puts emotions into words we have in common. Read the rest of this psalm, or any Scripture God lays on your heart, and follow these simple steps to add it to daily prayer.

1. *Highlight and Take Notes*

Highlight repetitive phrases and words, and anything that speaks to a current life circumstance. Also, organize notes for yourself. Find a way to flag what stands out, for reference when you are reviewing or meditating.

2. *Explore Study Bible Notes, Bible Dictionaries, and Commentaries*

Study Bibles and apps are rich with resources that bring biblical prayers to life. Follow trails of verses as if God is leading the way through a personal hike in the Scriptural woods. Worry less about remembering it all and focus more on what He reveals along the way.

3. *Pray It*

Personalize the Scripture into a daily prayer and start to include it daily. Write prayers down, print out verses, and copy them into a journal. Switch the pronouns to make them more personal. A prayer King David prayed can become a personal prayer, or a simple note from Scripture. Prayer is personal. Biblical examples are just that, examples. The most important thing is to keep the conversation going.

> *He set the earth on its foundations,*
> *never to be moved.*
> *You covered it with the deep like a garment;*
> *the waters stood above the mountains.*
> *At Your rebuke the waters fled;*
> *at the sound of Your thunder they hurried away—*
> *the mountains rose and the valleys sank*
> *to the place You appointed for them—*
> *You set a boundary they cannot cross;*
> *they will never again cover the earth.*
> (Psalm 104:5-9)

In the search to heal what ails us, there are plenty of worldly solutions claiming to right wrongs and undo hurts. But, today's verse reminds us of God's sovereign healing. He secures the world. God set the borders of the ocean and perimeters of the sky, the depths of the ocean and heights of mountainous ranges. The sun rises and the sun sets, day after day, dependably.

Throughout my Christian life, I have been taught the importance of prayer to which my family and I are beneficiaries of that. During the year of 2001, my husband lost his liver: within a month's time, our God made it possible for him to be a recipient from a donor, which happened to be same blood type, size, and all. To this day, he's still living with that liver. We are grateful to the Almighty God for His faithfulness toward us. On a daily basis, one is fed from Isaiah 58:8-9: "We will call upon His Name and He will answer." So true. In all that, faith is the key.

When you pray, it's probably because you want something to change. If you are praying for a blessing, you want to feel blessed afterward. When you pray for protection, you want to feel safe. When you pray for deliverance, you want your problems to go away as soon as possible; or if change doesn't happen like you think it should, you might conclude that praying doesn't really work.

That's probably why God has filled the Bible with stories of answered prayers. People implored God to intercede in their messy lives, which, of course, He did. As you read these incredible stories of answered prayers, notice two important aspects:

Max Lucado wrote this about God's power and control:

> What controls you doesn't control Him. What troubles you doesn't trouble Him. What fatigues you doesn't fatigue Him. Is an eagle disturbed by traffic? No, he rises above it. Is the whale perturbed by a hurricane? Of course not, he plunges beneath it. Is the lion flustered by the mouse standing directly in his way? No, he steps over it. How much more is God able to soar above, plunge beneath, and step over the troubles of the earth! As Matthew 19:26 tells us, "With men this is impossible, but with God all things are possible."

We need each other for comfort, and we benefit from the medicine the earth provides, but neither is as powerful as God's sovereign hand of love. It is a love Jesus died for us on the cross so that we may come to Him and be healed ... over and over again. When solutions seem senseless, look

Be Encouraged Through Prayer

to Him.(https://www.thomasnelsonbibles.com/wp-content/uploads/2016/12/Grace-for-the-Moment-Devotional.pdf)

THE ATTITUDE AND MOTIVES OF THE PERSON WHO PRAYED

The power With Which God Answered

These stories could change the way you pray and change how your prayers get answered:

1. Hannah is infertile, and she prays desperately for a son.

Hannah was the unfortunate, barren second wife, ridiculed and humiliated by the wife who easily bore children. So Hannah pleaded with God for a son, promising to give him back to the Lord: *"O Lord Almighty, if you will only look upon your servant's misery and remember me, and not forget your servant but give her a son, then I will give him to the Lord for all the days of his life"* (1 Sam. 11).

Sure enough, Samuel, her son, became the greatest prophet in Israel's history, who maintained direct communication with God throughout his life. In addition to Samuel, God gave Hannah three more sons and two daughters. When we are willing to give our best to God, He blesses us with more.

Be Encouraged Through Prayer

    2. Peter is in prison for preaching the gospel; the church prayed for his release.

After the Christian faith began to take root, Peter was arrested by King Herod and put him in prison. *"So Peter was kept in prison, but the church was earnestly praying to God for him"* (Acts 12:5). One night, an angel appeared in Peter's jail cell and led him out of the prison, through doors and past guards. Peter arrived at Mary's house, where the church was gathered praying; the servant girl was so surprised, she forgot to let him right in the house. Sometimes God answers our prayers so quickly, it surprises us.

    3. Jerusalem is under siege, so Hezekiah prays to save his people.

The powerful Assyrian king Sennacharib had laid siege to Jerusalem. King Hezekiah, who told his people to keep their faith in God, prayed for delivery from their enemy: *"And Hezekiah prayed to the Lord: 'Now, O Lord our God, deliver us from his hand, so that all kingdoms on earth may know that you alone, O Lord, are God'"* (1 Kings 19:20).

That night, the angel of the Lord killed 85,000 Assyrian soldiers, which compelled the rest of the army to return home without a fight. Whenever God's people follow His plan, He wages war on their behalf.

    4. Jairus asks Jesus to heal his daughter so she won't die.

Jairus, a synagogue ruler, risked his position in his faith community by making a request of the new religious teacher, Jesus, right in front of everyone: *"My little daughter is dying.*

Please come and put your hands on her so that she will be healed and live" (Mark 5:23).

Jesus tested Jairus's faith with a stop along the way to heal a sick woman, so before Jesus got to Jairus's house, the little girl had already died. But Jesus was planning more than a healing; He told Jairus to believe. Jesus entered the house and raised the girl back to life. Jesus wants to exceed our hearts' desires and wants to resurrect our faith.

5. Moses asks God to see Him.

Moses, called *"the friend of God"* (James 2:23), talked to God regularly. In a beautiful conversation, Moses asked for God's blessing on the Israelites and for God's presence to go with them as they traveled. Then Moses asked to see God's glory, God's very personage, up close: *"Now show me your glory"* (Exod. 33:18). God responded by tucking Moses into a little cleft on Mount Sinai and covering his view until God stood before him. Then God removed his hand and allowed Moses to view His form from the back. What was the result of this encounter? Moses so greatly resembled God's brilliance that he had to wear a veil over his face so the Israelites could look at him. How much of God's presence could we witness and represent, if we worshipped like Moses?

6. Hezekiah prays because God tells him that he is about to die.

When King Hezekiah became deathly ill, the prophet Isaiah came to him with a message from God that he would die. Hezekiah prayed and cried to God. *"Remember, O Lord, how I have walked before you faithfully and with* wholehearted devotion and have done what is good in your eyes" (2 Kings 20:3).

Before Isaiah had left the palace, God instructed him to return with a new message: *"I have heard your prayers and seen your tears; I will heal you… I will add 15 years to your life."* God responds to us when we remain in relationship with Him; He may even change His mind.

7. Jesus prays for God's will before His arrest and crucifixion.

The night of Jesus's betrayal, Jesus prayed alone in a garden, asking for God to protect His followers. Jesus agonized in prayer to God, saying, *"Father, if you are willing, take this cup from me; yet not my will, but yours be done"* (Luke 22:42).

May we learn to ask for God's mercy, even while we commit to obeying His will.

8. To save his life and his friends' lives, Daniel prays for God to reveal a dream and its interpretation.

When Babylonian King Nebuchadnezzar had a confusing dream, he ordered his counselors to describe the dream and tell him what it meant, or they would all die: *"Then Daniel returned to his house and explained the matter to his friends Hananiah, Mishael and Azariah. He urged them to plead for mercy from the God of heaven concerning this mystery, so that he and his friends might not be executed with the rest of the wise men of Babylon"* (Dan. 2:17-18).

Not only were Daniel and his friends saved, but they were also elevated to positions of high authority in this pagan country. Daniel would also become a spiritual influence to three powerful kings. You have no idea where God will place you, if you are willing to identify yourself as a praying believer who expects God to answer.

9. When Elisha and his servant are surrounded by the enemy, Elisha prays for God to reveal His power.

Elisha's prophetic abilities were defeating the plans of an enemy king, so the king sent a battalion to surround the city where Elisha was to launch an attack. As Elisha's servant panicked, Elisha prayed, *"O Lord, open his eyes so he may see"* (2 Kings 6:16). So God gave the servant the ability to see a vast army of heavenly hosts in fiery chariots, encircling the enemy. Then Elisha prayed for God to blind the enemy army, which He did. Next, Elisha led them away from the city. If we could see God's protective celestial army encircling us every day, realizing that they are blind to His power, we might have the faith to do whatever He asks of us.

10. A thief on a cross asks Jesus to save him before he dies.

While Jesus suffered on the cross to provide us salvation for our sins, two thieves hung next to him. While one of them ridiculed Jesus for allowing Himself to be crucified, the second asked for forgiveness: *"Then he said, 'Jesus, remember me when you come into your kingdom" Jesus answered him, 'I tell you the truth, today you will be with me in paradise'"* (Luke 23:42-43).

Jesus forgave the thief during His dying moments. It's never too late for a spiritual transformation.

I sure hope you understand the power of prayer. Yes, God knows what we need, but prayer is an act of humility. Jesus told us to ask, that our joy may be full (John 16:23, 24). Again, He told us to ask and we would receive. Every one who asks, receives (Matt. 7:7, 8). Don't forget. ASK!

To receiving answered prayer is to make every prayer, relative to what you've asked, a statement of faith instead of a statement of unbelief.

It is thinking faith thoughts and speaking faith words that leads the heart out of defeat into victory.

Unbelief and doubt will undo your prayers. Begin making faith confessions as part of your prayer life. A confession is a statement of agreement with God on a subject. For example, Psalm 23 is one of the favorites of many people. Instead of saying, "The Lord is my Shepherd. I shall not want," you can make a faith confession by saying, "The Lord is my Shepherd. I do not lack any good thing. I do not lack healing. I do not lack faith. I do not lack power. I do not lack good Christian friends of like precious faith. I do not lack finances. I have everything I need!"

That is a faith statement. You may not have these things, but Jesus said that when you pray, believe you will receive them and you shall have them! So, convert your prayers into statements of faith!

The short answer is yes; God wants to hear from us, and He promises that He will answer. He tells us to pray without ceasing. And God answers our prayer, but sometimes His answers aren't what we expect. Sometimes, they aren't what we want to hear, but they are always what we need and what is good for us. This is where it can get hard. To truly believe this, you must trust God, even when His answer seems so wrong. "All things work together for good to those who love the Lord." It's not always easy to see. Sometimes God even appears to be silent, but He does answer when you are ready to hear His answer. So, pray.

Pray when you are alone. Pray when you are struggling. Pray when you feel lost. Pray when you're happy. Pray when you're bored. Pray for yourself. Pray for others. Pray with others. But pray.

God will listen. He will open your eyes. He will open your ears. He will open your heart and He will answer. Or, follow the example of the Lord's Prayer. Jesus taught His followers a pattern for prayer that we call the Lord's Prayer. The language we use today when we say that prayer is quite formal.

Our Father who art in Heaven,
Hallow it be Thy name,
Thy Kingdom Come,
Thy will be done on Earth as it is in Heaven.
Give us this day our daily bread,
And forgive us our trespasses, as we forgive those who trespass against us,
And lead us not into temptation,
But deliver us from evil,
For thine is the Kingdom, and the power and the glory,
Forever and ever. Amen.

But, the message is really quite simple:
God, our heavenly Father; Your name is great.
Please bring Your kingdom into our lives,
and ensure that Your will is done and Your love is shown, so that earth will be like heaven.

Please, teach us to trust You to provide us with what we need, when we need it, and forgive us when we mess up.

We promise to forgive others when they mess up and hurt us.

Please, help us to avoid being tempted to do things that would hurt others or ourselves, and protect us from ourselves and those who would lead us into harm.

There's far more to prayer than the Lord's Prayer. Jesus gave it as an example to allow us to better understand our relationship with God. After all, prayer is about relationship

Be Encouraged Through Prayer

with God. Prayers don't need big words to be eloquent; sometimes, our prayer is just "Thanks" or "Help me." They just need to be honest and from the heart. That's it. Even when you're disappointed and frustrated with God, take it to him in prayer. He will listen (Jer.:12-13).

How to Fight Battles When Facing Spiritual Warfare

Prayer is work; it requires an all-out battle. Colossians 4:2 says we are to "continue earnestly in prayer." That's what it means to be a prayer warrior, facing problems on a daily basis. We're in a battle in this world. We may not see it; we might forget it's there, but the enemy would love nothing more than to fill our minds with discouragement and defeat. If you're a believer who is living like salt and light in a dark world, you won't go for long without encountering the obstacles and attacks he will hurl your direction. Though we can't stop his cruel attacks, we don't have to let him win. God reminds us in His Word to stay aware of Satan's schemes, to live alert in this world, and to stay close to Him.

God gives specific instructions in His Word. He gives us all we need to stand strong in this life. Yet, all too often we race through busy, full days, unprepared or simply not aware of what we're up against, or who the real enemy even is.

The forces of darkness don't wait for us to be ready for their attacks. They're ruthless, determined, and cunning. The devil couldn't care less if we feel prepared or prayed up for our day. In fact, he prefers when we're not.

But in a broken, dark world, how can we really know if we're just facing the expected difficulties of life or the attacks of the enemy? Jesus Himself told us that in this life we would experience troubles (John 16:33), so we know this to be true. Though many times we may not fully know who or what is behind the struggles, we can be assured that God equips us for battle, and He instructs us to live alert.

Spiritual warfare is not giving the devil more attention or focusing too much on his evil ways, whereas biblical warfare is making ourselves more attentive to what God is doing and remembering to stand firm and let Him fight our fiercest battles. There's power through His Spirit, His Word, and in prayer. We can be confident that He is always with us, leading our way and covering us from behind.

Tactics of the Devil

All day, every day, an invisible war rages around you—unseen, unheard, yet felt throughout every aspect of your life. A devoted, devilish enemy seeks to wreak havoc on everything that matters to you: your heart, your mind, your marriage, your children, your relationships, your resilience, your dreams, your destiny. But His battle plan depends on catching you unaware and unarmed. If you're tired of being pushed around, you need to stand up to the enemy through prayer by letting God fight your battles. The enemy always fails miserably when He meets a man/woman dressed for the occasion. *The Armor of God*, more than merely a biblical description of the believer's inventory, is an action plan for putting it on and developing a personalized strategy to secure victory. Know, as Christians we are always under the attacks of the devil.

Christian Spiritual Warfare: Cast Down Every Imagination

Our mind is the battlefield of spiritual warfare. Spiritual warfare is a battle for our minds between our evil imaginations and the glorious knowledge of God. The overall objective of spiritual warfare is to *"have the mind of Christ."* First Corinthians 2:16 defines the objective of spiritual warfare:

> I Corinthians 2:16: *"For who hath known the mind of the Lord that he may instruct him? But we have the mind of Christ."*

Christian Spiritual Warfare is a Fight of Faith

Christian spiritual warfare is all about faith. Christian faith and hope gives us the power to fight in order to have the mind of Christ and lay hold of eternal life. First Timothy 6:12 defines spiritual warfare as the good fight of faith.

> I Timothy 6:12: *"Fight the good fight of faith, lay hold on eternal life, whereunto thou art also called, and hast professed a good profession before many witnesses."*

Spiritual warfare focuses totally on conquering the human mind in order for us to take on and keep the mind of Christ. Spiritual warfare does not focus on the destruction of the devil, the flesh, enemies, the world, or death: these things are already defeated (Ps. 6:4). Psalm 6:4 advises us to rely on God to fight our spiritual battles.

> Psalm 6:4: *"Return, O LORD, deliver my soul: oh save me for thy mercies' sake."*

Losses and Troubles

This is a ruthless attack that Satan often brings against believers. It seems to come out of nowhere, and it's just one thing after another. It's hard to even see straight when you feel your life is suddenly spinning out of control. Job's life is an example to us of what this may be like (Job 1:2). The devil went to God to ask Him if he could torment Job, thinking he would try to lead him away from the Lord through many struggles. As we know from the book of Job, this just man stood strong. Though it seemed he was losing everything dear to him, he knew that God held him secure through all the loss and hardships.

God will never allow the enemy to have full control; he doesn't have the final say over our lives. We may face battles and attacks in this world, but we can trust in our mighty God to be our shelter through it all.

Attacks of Physical Danger We know from God's Word that the enemy wants nothing more than to "*steal, kill, and destroy*" our lives and all we love (John 10:10). He is a thief, a roaring lion, and preys on God's people. He desires to silence our voices and take us out of this world to shut off the light of God's love and hope through Christ. Many of us may have experienced near-death experiences, sudden and terrible illnesses, or holding loved ones who were at the brink of heaven. And yet God intervened to keep us here longer. There are many stories in the Bible of God's people under great physical attack and danger, and so many miracles that God performed to bring them safely through. Even when it didn't make sense; even when it seemed to be the end.

Daniel faced lions in the lion's den (Dan. 6). His attackers thought he'd be gone by morning, but God intervened and shut the mouth of every lion. Be assured, God is still shutting mouths today. If you're facing attacks, and feel your life has been threatened, our God is a miracle worker. The Bible reminds us that our times are in His hands. We can be confident that He knows every day we are to be here on earth, and He will keep us, and our loved ones, safely in His care until He calls us home to heaven. There's no reason to fear; stand strong through prayer and His word.

Increase Temptation

Though we live with daily struggles and temptations all around us, many times there are spiritual attacks on our lives that put us at greater risk to go astray. It is a battle, a ruthless one, and the enemy will fight hard against us. He desires not only to bring us down, but also all those around us. He loves to see news stories splashed across headlines of believers who have fallen, who have made terrible choices of sin. He loves disunity among Christians and wants nothing more than to break up families and every relationship we hold dear. We must stand strong and stay aware. Don't give him a foothold into your life; don't give him even an inch of room. He'll come in and wreak havoc, and try to lead us astray faster than we even know what happened.

Often when we find ourselves weary, already weakened, we're on his radar. Jesus, Himself, is our greatest example of this when He faced the devil's temptation in the wilderness (Matt. :1-11) He was fasting; He was hungry; He was physically weakened and tired, and, of course, the enemy jumped on that time to bring on the temptations to a greater degree than ever. One slip-up is all he was looking for. One wrong move. One "yes" to sin. But Jesus stood strong and resisted His attacks, every single one. He spoke God's Word out loud. He held fast to truth and stepped over Satan's vicious lies and attacks. And He leads us to the same today. Don't be taken unaware. When you start sensing strong pulls away from God's truth and ways, you can know who is at the bottom of it all.

Feelings of Overwhelming Despair

Many may struggle with anxiety and fear in this life. Many may be facing depression and mood disorders, or mental illness. But often the attacks of spiritual forces against our lives raises the intensity to an even greater degree than normal day-to-day struggles. It's ruthless, unrelenting; we feel alone and completely overwhelmed and stuck in deep fear and despair. Recognize this darkness for what it is and stand strong!

This is where Satan will lead some to even contemplate taking their lives or making choices they never would have thought they'd make. It's a cruel trap, but there's hope from the pit because of Christ. He is the One who can lift us straight out of that darkness. He is the One who can calm our fears and give us strength we didn't even know was possible.

Elijah the prophet was a great man of God. He had led the battle against false idols and resisted those who stood against God. In all eyes, he was a hero, respected and honored. And yet, right after such great victory and success, he faced extreme warfare. He ran for his life, in fear. Despair and darkness had gripped his life and he couldn't even think straight. It seemed that he'd forgotten everything God had just done on behalf of his people (1 Kings 19). But here's what I love about God – He came to him right where he was. He provided for him. He took care of him. He strengthened him. He gave great mercy and grace to him. And then He did this — He called him to action. He gave him a plan to keep moving forward. He still had great purpose for the prophet in the coming days; there was still work to be done. And He does the same for us today too. If you find yourself running scared or stuck in despair, stop long enough to think through who you're really running from. Don't buy into the enemy's pursuit and attacks. He has no lasting power over you, and God will hold you strong for the road still ahead.

Feelings of Condemnation and Guilt

This one can be difficult to see through at times, because this attack can be so subtle and can happen slowly over time. But when we stop and look closely, we can call it out for what it is. A slow, constant pulling away from God's truth will leave us feeling confused, irritated, conflicted, and facing generalized feelings of guilt and condemnation that we just can't seem to shake off. We've lost our desire to even press in and pray. Or we're too busy; we've got too much to do, even good things. We're not in God's Word. We're out of fellowship with believers, somehow believing the lie we can do this life thing all on our own. And yet we feel a dark cloud of confusion and guilt that follows us around and won't go away. Bitterness can set in; conflict and broken relationships that we once cared about. We don't even know what to believe anymore and have started listening more to what the world says is right.

Get out of this trap now, wake up! Stir yourself to action and know that God's power is greater to break through that trap of condemnation and confusion. God reminds us in His Word that He is *"not the author of confusion but of peace"* (1 Cor. 14:33). He tells us that *"there is no condemnation for those who are in Christ Jesus"* (Rom. 8:1).

His Spirit will bring conviction over sin to His children. He will draw us to Himself and show us what we need to make right. But within that, there is great hope and grace. It is not a ruthless, condemning voice. It is not the lies and heaping on of guilt that the enemy will attempt to wreak havoc over us. Step away from that dark cloud and into God's light and truth.

God's Battle Plan for Us when Facing Spiritual Warfare

God arms us with the sword, the Word of God, to stand against the enemy's lies. He equips us with strength, wisdom, and discernment through His own Spirit to stay strong in the battle. He invites us to spend time in His presence, through prayer and worship, pressing in to know Him more.

As we grow to know God's truth more and more, understanding what is real, we also grow to know more what is false. We're able to quickly discern when something's not right. We are stronger to stand against it in the powerful name of Jesus. He never leaves us to fend for ourselves in a dark world, but reminds us He is constantly with us, fighting for us, even when we cannot see.

God offers us some suggestions to stand firm from the attack of the enemy:

The gift of the Holy Spirit

God fills us with strength, wisdom, and discernment through His own Spirit to stay strong in the battle. He never leaves us to fend for ourselves and fight in our own strength. We need His fresh filling every day; we need the empowerment only He can offer. Every believer has the gift of God's Spirit dwelling within them. The same power that raised Lazarus from the dead, parted the sea, broke open prison doors, and caused the lame to walk is the same powerful Spirit still alive and at work within us today.

> "But you will receive power when the Holy Spirit comes on you; and you will be my witnesses in Jerusalem, and in all Judea and Samaria, and to the ends of the earth" (**Acts 1:8**).

> "The Spirit helps us in our weakness. For we do not know what to pray for as we ought, but the Spirit himself intercedes for us with groanings too deep for words." (**Romans 8: 26**)

Armor of God

God reminds us not to go into the day without being prepared and equipped for battle. He tells us to take up His full armor in order to stand against the enemy's schemes. Each piece has a specific purpose and is designed for our protection and covering. Just as a soldier would not go to battle unprepared, we also should be fully ready for the attacks we will face.

> *Put on the full armor of God, that you may be able to stand against the schemes of the devil. For our struggle is not against flesh and blood, but against the rulers, against the powers, against the world forces of this darkness, against the spiritual forces of wickedness in the heavenly places. Take up the full armor of God, so that you will be able to resist in the evil day, and having done everything, to stand firm. Stand firm therefore, having girded your loins with truth, and having put on the breastplate*

> *of righteousness, and having shod your feet with the preparation of the gospel of peace, in addition to all, taking up the shield of faith with which you will be able to extinguish all the flaming arrows of the evil one. And take the helmet of salvation and the sword of the Spirit, which is the word of God.* **(Ephesians 6:11-17)**

Prayer

God invites us to have a relationship with Him. He desires for us to spend time in His presence, pressing in to know Him more. He reminds us constantly in His word of the importance of prayer and the power that is found there. He tells us to **<u>pray without ceasing</u>**. And even when we don't know what to say, He tells us that the Spirit intercedes for us. He never leaves us to fend for ourselves in a dark world, but reminds us that He is constantly with us, fighting for us, even when we cannot see.

> *"And pray in the Spirit on all occasions, with all kinds of prayers and requests. With this in mind, be alert and always keep on praying for all the saints."* **(Ephesians 6:18)**

> *"...The effective prayer of a righteous man can accomplish much."* **(James 5:16)**

His Word

He arms us with the sword of the Spirit, *the **Word of God***, to stand against the enemy's lies. Praying God's words back to Him is a powerful weapon against the forces of evil. It is truth going out into enemy territory. It reminds us that God knows our way and understands what we face today. It builds our faith and our trust in God. It guards our hearts and focuses our minds back on Him.

> *"For the word of God is living and active, sharper than any two-edged sword, piercing to the division of soul and of spirit, of joints and of marrow, and discerning the thoughts and intentions of the heart."* ***(Hebrews 4:12)***

> *"All Scripture is breathed out by God and profitable for teaching, for reproof, for correction, and for training in righteousness."* ***(2 Timothy 3:16)***

Power of Praise

Praise invites God's presence. He dwells close to us when we praise Him. And praise is a powerful weapon as well. It makes the enemy flee. It pushes back the darkness that surrounds and blocks the attacks and hissing lies over us. Evil will not stick around if we're praising our God, who will fight our battles for us. In the story of Jehoshaphat, we see God miraculously defeat the enemy, because of the people's obedience to praise Him.

> "As they began to sing and praise, the Lord set ambushes against the men of Ammon and Moab and Mount Seir who were invading Judah, and they were defeated" (**2 Chron. 20:22**). "He inhabits the praises of His people" (**Ps. 22:**).

Obedience to Christ

Our willingness to obey the words and commandments of Christ in a world that would say to walk our own way is huge. It sets a powerful example that says we are willing to die to our own desires and live for the glory of God. But it will never happen naturally. Our very flesh, our own desires and sin nature, will fight against it every step of the way. It's a daily choice that says we will be careful of every thought; we will take up our cross daily and follow Christ's ways, not our own.

Submit to God's authority. Be ruthless with sin, which is an open door for the enemy to work. Resist him and he has to flee.

> "Submit yourselves, then, to God. Resist the devil, and he will flee from you." (**James 4:**). "We destroy arguments and every lofty opinion raised against the knowledge of God, and take **every thought captive** to obey Christ," (**2 Cor 10:5**).

The Blood of Christ and the Word of Our Testimony

We are overcomers in this life because He has overcome. And our lives are hidden in Christ with God. No enemy or obstacle can touch our souls. When we have been set free by the blood of Christ and the power of His sacrifice by death on the Cross, we have a new identity in Him. We've been bought with a price; we are not our own, but covered by the grace and forgiveness of Jesus. We live victorious, and no demons or darkness can ever separate us from the love of God, which is in Christ our Lord. There is power in the name of Jesus.

> *"And they overcame him because of the blood of the Lamb and because of the word of their testimony, and they did not love their life even when faced with death."* **(Revelation 12:11)**

> *"For the word of the cross is folly to those who are perishing, but to us who are being saved it is the power of God."* **(1 Corinthians1:18)**

When we belong to Christ, the enemy never has the final word over our lives. We are secure in God's hands.

Press on, be courageous and free and never held back by fear or defeat. The battle belongs to the Lord, and He has the final victory!

In conclusion, God wants you to remember what to do when life is hard.

In the grand scheme of things, a stressful period doesn't impact life or eternity all that much, but in those longer seasons of joblessness, financial stress, marriage strain, and other ongoing life events, the stress and frustration can seem overwhelming. Below are four things I've learned to remember in those challenging seasons of life that have helped me and I pray they help you as well!

Struggles in life are inevitable, but destruction is optional. Remembering these four principles can make all the difference:

1. Remember that your character should always be stronger than your circumstances.

We can't always control what happens to us, but we can always control how we choose to respond. In those moments when I choose to stop complaining and instead give thanks to God for the good in my life, the parts that seem bad start to seem much less significant. Choose to keep a positive attitude and thankful heart, regardless of what you're going through.

> *"Rejoice always, pray continually, give thanks in all circumstances; for this is God's will for you in Christ Jesus."* **(1 Thessalonians 5:16-18)**

2. Remember that your struggles always lead to strength.

Every difficulty in your life, whether big or small, is something God will use to produce more strength, faith, and perseverance in you, if you let Him! All your pain has a purpose.

> *"And we know that in all things God works for the good of those who love him, who have been called according to his purpose."* **(Romans 8:28)**

3. Remember that God's timing is always perfect.

God's plans are almost always different from our plans, but His plans are always perfect! Have the patience to wait on His timing, instead of forcing your own.

> "For I know the plans I have for you declares the Lord; plans to prosper you and not to harm you, plans to give you hope and a future." **(Jeremiah 29:11)**

4. Remember that God will never leave your side.

You may feel like you're going through this struggle all alone, but from the moment you ask Jesus to bring you into God's family, He will be by your side to the end, so never lose hope!

> "Be strong and courageous. Do not be afraid or terrified because of them, for the Lord your God goes with you; he will never leave you nor forsake you." **(Deuteronomy 31:6)**

Father, we praise You for the delicate way You powerfully align our lives to Your creation. Thank you for the waters and mountains that remind us of You. Forgive us for overlooking Your presence in every aspect of our lives, and bless us to notice and give glory to You, for You are our healer. In Jesus's name, Amen.